Start with Art

Textiles

Isabel Thomas

www.raintreepublishers.co.uk
Visit our website to find out more information about Raintree books.

To order:
☎ Phone 0845 6044371
📠 Fax +44 (0) 1865 312263
💻 Email myorders@raintreepublishers.co.uk

Customers from outside the UK please telephone +44 1865 312262

Raintree is an imprint of Capstone Global Library Limited, a company incorporated in England and Wales having its registered office at 7 Pilgrim Street, London, EC4V 6LB – Registered company number: 6695582

Edited by Dan Nunn, Rebecca Rissman, and Catherine Veitch
Designed by Richard Parker
Picture research by Mica Brancic and Hannah Taylor
Originated by Capstone Global Library
Printed and bound in China by South China Printing Company Ltd

ISBN 978 1 406 22738 3
15 14 13 12 11
10 9 8 7 6 5 4 3 2 1

British Library Cataloguing in Publication Data
Thomas, Isabel
Textiles. -- (Start with art)
746-dc22
A full catalogue record for this book is available from the British Library.

Acknowledgements
We would like to thank the following for permission to reproduce photographs: Alamy Images pp. 6 (© V&A Images), 17 (© Hemis); © Capstone Publishers pp. 4, 20, 21, 22 (Karon Dubke); Corbis pp. 5 (© Hamid Sardar), 8 (Bloomimage), 11 (Jon Hicks), 14 (Kazuyoshi Nomachi), 16 (Martin Harvey), 18 (Gianni Dagli Orti); Getty Images p. 13 (Ariel Skelley); Photolibrary pp. 10, 23 – fibres, 23 – yarn (Photononstop/ Paul Vilcot); Rex Features p. 15 (Richard Sowersby); Scala pp. 9 (MOMA, New York), 19 (Art Resource/ The Newark Museum); Shutterstock pp. 12 (© Lagui), 23 – create (© Monkey Business Images), 23 – embroidered (© Royik Yevgen), 23 – loom (© fenghui), 23 – symbols (© qushe), 23 – weave (© Losevsky Pavel); The Bridgeman Art Library p. 7 (Agnew's, London, UK).

Front cover photograph of a man weaving ikat, Lombok, Indonesia reproduced with permission of Getty Images (© Bruno Morandi). Back cover photograph of textiles reproduced with permission of © Capstone Publishers (Karon Dubke). Back cover photograph of weaving reproduced with permission of © Capstone Publishers (Karon Dubke).

Contents

Some words are shown in bold, **like this**. You can find out what they mean by looking in the glossary.

What are textiles?

Textiles are materials made from **fibres** or **yarns**.

There are many different kinds of textiles.

People have made textiles for thousands of years.

People make textiles for clothes, furniture, and many other things.

Why do people make textiles?

Every part of the world has special types of textiles.

This textile was made in England. Can you name any of the plants and birds?

People also use textiles to **create** art.

Textiles can show ideas or tell a story.

Where can I see textiles?

Textiles are all around you.

Clothes can show who we are, what we do, and where we come from.

Museums collect textiles from different times and places.

Visit a museum to look at art made from textiles.

What do people use to make textiles?

yarn

Natural **fibres** come from plants or animals.

The fibres are twisted together to make **yarn**.

Most human-made fibres are made
from oil.

Human-made fibres can be used to make
some textiles such as waterproof materials.

How do people make textiles?

There are different ways to turn **yarn** into textiles.

Cotton or silk threads can be twisted together to make lace.

Wool yarn can be looped together by knitting.

People also **weave** yarn to make cloth.

What is weaving?

loom

People use a **loom** to **weave** textiles.

Weaving can be done by hand, or by a machine.

One thread is passed in and out of another, to lock them together.

Overlapping the threads makes woven textiles strong.

How do people decorate textiles?

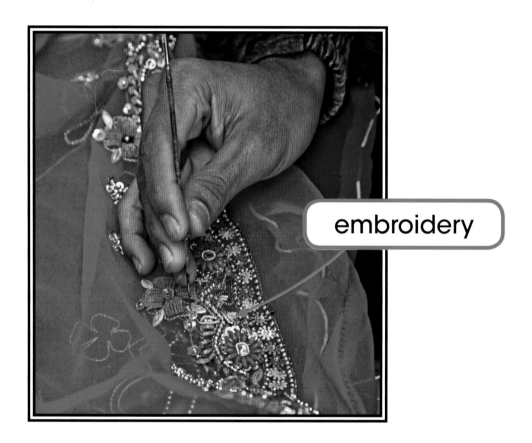

embroidery

Dyes and prints add colours and patterns to textiles.

Embroidery gives textiles interesting textures.

Patterns and colours can have special meanings.

The **symbols** on this Tapa cloth are important to the people who made it.

How can textiles tell a story?

The Bayeux Tapestry tells the story of a famous battle.

The pictures are **embroidered** on to the cloth using a needle and wool thread.

The patterns on this cloth from Africa are made with blue dye.

In Africa, the **symbols** are passed down through families.

Start to make textiles!

Many artists **create** art from things that they find. Try making a recycled **weaving**.

1. Collect long strips of magazines and newspapers, packaging, ribbon, string, plastic bags, and wrapping paper.

2. Choose colours and textures that remind you of the seaside or jungle.

3. Draw a line along each end of a piece of thick paper. Cut the paper into strips, stopping at the lines.

4. Weave your recycled strips under and over the paper strips. Push each strip up to the top before you weave the next one.

5. Cover the back of your **weaving** with sticky tape to hold all the strips together.

6. Trim the ends of the strips to finish your woven art.

Glossary

create make something using your own ideas and how you feel inside

embroidered decorated by using a needle and thread to sew pictures, patterns, beads, or mirrors on to cloth

fibres very small pieces of natural or human-made materials that can be used to make textiles

loom machine for weaving yarn into fabric

symbols pictures with a special meaning

weave make by pulling threads in and out of each other

yarn fibres that have been twisted together to make a long thread

Find out more

Websites

On this website you can design your own textile story:
www.bayeuxtapestry.org.uk/interactive/BayeuxCreate.htm

Invent a textile pattern on this website:
www.vam.ac.uk/vastatic/microsites/1231_vivienne_westwood/
tartan.html

Index